US Midwest Style

Recipes

A Cookbook of Dish Ideas from the

American Heartland!

BY - Julia Chiles

OOOOOOOOOOOOOOOOOOOOOOOOOOOOOOOOOOOOOOOOO

License Notes

No part of this Book can be reproduced in any form or by any means including print, electronic, scanning or photocopying unless prior permission is granted by the author.

All ideas, suggestions and guidelines mentioned here are written for informative purposes. While the author has taken every possible step to ensure accuracy, all readers are advised to follow information at their own risk. The author cannot be held responsible for personal and/or commercial damages in case of misinterpreting and misunderstanding any part of this Book

OOOOOOOOOOOOOOOOOOOOOOOOOOOOOOOOOOOOOO

Table of Contents

Introduction

Do you marvel at the variety in the types of meals served in the American Midwest?

Would you enjoy creating some of these recipes at home?

Can you source local ingredients or substitutes to make authentic Midwestern dishes?

Typical meals in the Midwest are often called "All American." They include meatloaf, hamburgers, steaks or roast beef, accompanied by veggies like corn on the cob, green beans or potatoes. Dessert is often apple or cherry pie, but cakes are served, as well.

Midwesterners often prepare meat or chicken pot pies, which include meat and veggies baked inside a pastry crust. They also enjoy potato salad and wild rice soup.

People in the heartland of the United States usually partake in three meals per day, with the largest being dinner. They snack more than many people in other countries between meals, too.

Breakfasts may include sausage or bacon with eggs, or oatmeal or grits, each sometimes served with biscuits or toast. It's not uncommon for Midwesterners to just grab a roll or doughnut with their coffee, either, on the way out the door for work or school.

Lunch in Middle America can consist of sandwiches, soups or salad. Hamburgers and fries are popular fast food lunches or dinners. For a taste of the US Midwest, read on…

Breakfast in the Midwest is sometimes hurried, but if you have time, here are some super recipes...

Turkey Breakfast Quiche

This is a turkey-based version of classic quiche. It combines breast turkey meat, smoked, along with eggs and Swiss cheese. It's wonderful, especially when served with fresh fruit.

Makes 6 Servings

Cooking + Prep Time: 40 minutes + 10 minutes cooking time

Ingredients:

- 1 x 9" pastry shell, unbaked
- 1 1/4 cups of diced, smoked, cooked turkey breast
- 1/3 cup of onion, chopped
- 1 tbsp. of butter, unsalted
- 1 to 1 1/2 cups of Swiss cheese shreds
- 3 slightly beaten eggs, large
- 1 cup of cream, light
- 1/2 tsp. of mustard, dry
- 1/8 tsp. of salt, kosher
- A dash of red pepper, ground

Instructions:

1. Bake pastry shell at 450F for four to five minutes, till it starts puffing. Remove it from the oven. Reduce temperature of oven to 375F.

2. Cook turkey with onions in skillet on med-high till onion becomes tender but has not yet browned. Sprinkle the cheese over the bottom of baked shell. Spoon the turkey mixture over the cheese.

3. Whisk eggs, cream, mustard, salt red pepper together in medium sized bowl. Pour this over turkey-cheese mixture.

4. Bake quiche at 375F for 25-30 minutes, till knife pushed into mixture near middle comes back clean. Allow quiche to cool for 8-10 minutes and serve.

Buckwheat Blueberry Pancakes

These pancakes are made from buckwheat, which is a whole grain. It Makes them low in sodium and low in fat. The blueberries give them a pleasing, sweet taste.

Makes 6 Servings

Cooking + Prep Time: 55 minutes

Ingredients:

- 1/2 cup of flour, buckwheat
- 1/2 cup of flour, whole wheat
- 1 tbsp. of sugar, granulated
- 1/2 tsp. of baking powder, low sodium
- 1/4 tsp. of baking soda, low sodium
- 1/4 tsp. of salt, kosher
- 1 slightly beaten egg, large
- 1 1/4 cup of butter milk, reduced sodium
- 1 tbsp. of oil, cooking
- 1/4 tsp. of vanilla, pure
- 3/4 cup of blueberries, frozen/thawed or fresh

Instructions:

1. Stir both flours, sugar, baking soda, baking powder and kosher salt together in medium sized bowl. Make indentation in middle of this mixture. Set bowl aside.
2. Slightly beat the egg and stir in the oil, vanilla and butter milk. Add this mixture in one dump to flour mixture. Stir till barely combined and still a bit lumpy. Then stir in the blueberries.
3. Heat skillet on med. heat. Pour 1/4 cup of batter for each individual pancake onto the hot griddle. Spread batter in circles that are four inches in diameter.
4. Cook on med. heat till pancakes turn light brown. Cook one to two minutes each side. Serve promptly.

Bacon, Egg Ham Hash

This recipe is a true family favorite. It includes bacon, eggs, ham and potatoes in a hearty and simple meal that is as good for brunch as it is for breakfast.

Makes 4 Servings

Cooking + Prep Time: 40 minutes

Ingredients:

- 4 slices of bacon
- 2 peeled, chopped potatoes, large
- Oil, cooking
- 8 oz. of chopped ham
- 5 lightly beaten eggs, large
- 1/4 tsp. of salt, kosher
- 1/8 tsp. of pepper, ground
- 1 ounce of cheddar cheese shreds

Instructions:

1. Cook bacon till crisp in large sized skillet and reserve the fat. Remove bacon. Drain on layered paper towels. Crumble and set bacon aside.

2. Add the potatoes to reserved bacon fat. Cook without covering on med. heat 8-10 minutes, till potatoes are browned and nearly tender, turning them frequently. Add ham. Cook for five to six more minutes, till potatoes are fully tender, while gently stirring.

3. Combine the eggs, kosher salt ground pepper in small sized bowl. Pour the egg mixture over the ham and potato mixture. Cook without stirring on med. heat till egg mixture starts setting around edges and on bottom. Lift and fold egg mixture, allowing uncooked egg to flow under it.

4. Continue to cook on med. heat till egg mixture has cooked fully, but still appears moist and glossy. Sprinkle with reserved bacon, then the cheese. Remove mixture from heat. Cover. Allow to stand for a minute or two, till cheese melts. Serve.

Easy Cinnamon Rolls

Not many people have unlimited time to make breakfast in the morning. This recipe uses pudding mix and frozen bread dough to make rolls that taste as good as homemade.

Makes 12 Servings

Cooking + Prep Time: 50 minutes + 40 minutes standing time + overnight chilling time

Ingredients:

- 1 x 12-count pkg. of cinnamon rolls cream cheese frosting, frozen
- 1 x 4-serving-sized pkg. of pudding mix, vanilla flavored or butterscotch
- 1/3 cup of brown sugar, packed
- 1/2 cup of melted butter, unsalted

Instructions:

1. Arrange the frozen rolls on pre-greased 10" x 15" x 1" pan. Chill frosting packets till you need them. Sprinkle the dry pudding mix on frozen rolls.
2. Whisk butter and brown sugar together in small sized bowl. Spoon some butter and sugar mixture over the rolls. Cover with wax paper and then cling wrap. Cover. Chill the rolls overnight.
3. Next day, remove cling wrap and wax paper. Allow to sit without refrigeration for 40-45 minutes.
4. Bake at 350F for 20-25 minutes till golden in color. Remove the pan from oven. Allow rolls to cool in the pan for five minutes or so. Invert the rolls on serving tray. Frost while warm. Serve.

Spring Veggie Scramble

Scrambles are the perfect quick breakfast, because you can adapt them to any season. Use vegetables that are in season for the time of year to make a creative, tasty breakfast.

Makes 3 Servings

Cooking + Prep Time: 25 minutes

Ingredients:

- 8 eggs, large
- 1 tbsp. of fresh dill, snipped
- Salt, kosher
- Pepper, ground
- 1 tbsp. of butter, unsalted
- 1 cored, chopped fennel bulb, small
- 1/2 cup of shelled peas
- 3 or 4 sliced radishes
- 1/4 cup of feta cheese crumbles

Instructions:

1. Whisk eggs, salt, pepper and dill together in medium sized bowl.

2. In large sized skillet, melt butter on med. heat. Add fennel. Cook till tender, five minutes or so. Add and stir in the radishes and peas. Cook for two to three minutes more, till barely crisp-tender.

3. Add eggs. Cook but do not stir till mixture starts setting around the edges and on bottom. Fold egg scramble so egg not yet cooked will be on bottom layer in pan.

4. Continue to cook on med. heat for three to four minutes, till egg mixture cooks through. Remove it from heat. Add feta and stir. Serve.

The Midwest includes large cities like Chicago and more, along with smaller towns and rural, farm areas for miles. There are wonderful lunch, dinner, side dish and appetizer recipes from many areas. Try one soon...

Midwest Meatloaf

Life in the Midwest US is as fast as it is in most other places, so convenience in recipes is a definite plus. This kid-friendly dinner uses local oats mixed into a pork and beef blend.

Makes 6 Servings

Cooking + Prep Time: 1 hour 25 minutes

Ingredients:

- 1 1/2 lbs. of ground beef, lean
- 1 cup of tomato sauce or juice
- 3/4 cups of uncooked Quaker oats, old-fashioned or quick
- 1 lightly beaten egg, large
- 1/4 cup of onion, chopped
- 1/2 tsp. of salt, kosher
- 1/4 tsp. of pepper, ground

Instructions:

1. Preheat oven to 350F.
2. Combine all ingredients in large sized bowl. Mix well but lightly. Press into 4" x 8" loaf pan.
3. Bake for an hour till done medium. Thermometer pushed in middle should show 160F. It should not be pink anymore, and the juices should be running clear. Allow to set for five minutes. Drain off juices before you slice and serve.

Lemon-Battered Fish

This is a favorite fish recipe for many in the heartland of the US. Lake Michigan, Lake Erie and countless local lakes and rivers provide many kinds of freshwater fish that make wonderful dishes.

Makes 6 Servings

Cooking + Prep Time: 1/2 hour

Ingredients:

- 1 1/2 cups of flour, all-purpose
- 1 tsp. of baking powder, low sodium
- 3/4 tsp. of salt, kosher
- 1/2 tsp. of sugar, granulated
- 1 lightly beaten egg, large
- 2/3 cup of water, filtered
- 2/3 cup of lemon juice, fresh if available
- 2 lbs. of walleye or perch fillets, sliced to make 1-serving pieces

To fry: oil

Optional: lemon wedges

Instructions:

1. Combine a cup of flour along with baking powder, kosher salt granulated sugar in a bowl.
2. In separate bowl, combine water, 1/3 cup of lemon juice and egg. Stir into the dry mixture till it is smooth.
3. Place remaining flour and lemon juice in shallow, medium bowls. Dip the fillets in the lemon juice, then the flour. Coat with the egg mixture.
4. Heat one inch of oil on med-high in large sized skillet. Fry the fillets till golden brown in color and easily flaked with fork. Drain on a layer of paper towels. Serve with some lemon wedges, if you like.

Deep Dish Chicago-Style Pizza

There are lots of places to eat deep-dish pizza, but the Chicago version is an icon of the Midwest. If you aren't traveling to the Windy City, you can make one at home.

Makes 12 Servings

Cooking + Prep Time: 1 hour 25 minutes

Ingredients:

For dough

- 2 1/2 cups of flour, all-purpose
- 1 x 1/4-oz. pkg. of yeast, quick-rising
- 1 1/2 tsp. of sugar, granulated
- 1 cup of water, filtered
- 1/3 cup of oil, olive
- 1/4 cup of corn meal

For topping

- 4 tsp. of oil, olive
- 1/2-lb. of mushrooms, sliced
- 1 x 28-oz. can of well-drained tomatoes, diced
- 1 x 8-oz. can of tomato sauce, low sodium
- 1 x 6-oz. can of tomato paste, reduced sodium
- 3 minced garlic cloves
- 1/2 tsp. of salt, kosher
- 1/4 tsp. of basil, dried
- 1/4 tsp. of oregano, dried
- 1/4 tsp. of pepper, ground
- 3 cups of mozzarella cheese shreds, part-skim
- 1 lb. of cooked, crumbled Italian sausage, bulk

Optional:

- 24 pepperoni slices
- 1/2 cup of Parmesan cheese, grated

Optional:

- basil leaves, sliced thinly

Instructions:

1. To prepare the dough, combine 1 1/2 cups of flour, corn meal, sugar, yeast and kosher salt. Heat oil and water to 120-130F in small sauce pan.
2. Add oil and water to dry ingredients. Beat till moistened lightly. Stir in remaining flour sufficient to form soft dough.
3. Turn the dough on floured work surface. Knead till elastic and smooth, usually six to eight minutes or so. Place in pre-greased bowl and turn once to grease top. Cover. Allow to sit in warm area and rise till size doubles, usually 1/2 hour.
4. Preheat the oven to 450F.

5. Cook mushrooms while stirring in 2 tsp. oil in large sized skillet on med-high till tender. Mix tomatoes, tomato paste, tomato sauce, garlic cloves and the seasonings in small bowl.

6. Grease 13" x 9" baking dish generously with 2 tsp. of oil. Uncover the dough. Punch it down on lightly floured work surface and roll out in 15" x 11" rectangle. Transfer this to the dish. Press into bottom and 1/2-way up sides. Use 2 cups of mozzarella cheese shreds to sprinkle.

7. Spoon 1/2 of sauce over cheese. Layer with sautéed mushrooms, sausage and pepperoni, if using. Top with Parmesan cheese and the rest of the mozzarella cheese shreds.

8. Cover dish. Bake for 30-35 minutes. Remove cover. Bake for five or six minutes more, till browned lightly. Sprinkle using basil, as desired. Serve.

Barbeque Brats

They love their brats in Wisconsin, and there are many ways to prepare them. This simple recipe is very popular, and always a hit at cookouts and tailgate parties.

Makes 10 Servings

Cooking + Prep Time: 3 1/2 hours

Ingredients:

- 10 links of bratwurst, uncooked
- 1 1/2 cups of broth, chicken or 1 x 12-oz. bottle of beer
- 1 cup of ketchup, low sodium
- 1 cup of BBQ sauce, honey
- 10 split buns, hot dog sized
- Mustard, spicy brown

Instructions:

1. Cover the brats and grill on oiled rack on med-high. Turn frequently, then transfer them to a large slow cooker.
2. Mix beer or broth, BBQ sauce and ketchup in large sized bowl. Pour the mixture over brats. Cover again and cook over low heat till cooked fully through. Place brats on the buns. Serve with brown mustard.

Breaded Tenderloin Sandwich

It's hard to improve on a pounded, breaded pork tenderloin, but this recipe does it. It adds a bun and some tasty Dijon mustard for a real treat.

Makes 4 Servings

Cooking + Prep Time: 50 minutes

Ingredients:

- 1 lb. of trimmed pork tenderloin
- Salt, kosher
- Pepper, ground
- 2 eggs, large
- 1 tsp. of garlic powder
- 1 tbsp. of mustard, Dijon
- 1 cup of Ritz® crackers or similar, crushed
- Oil, canola
- Kaiser rolls
- To garnish: onion slices, yellow mustard, sliced dill pickles

Instructions:

1. Cut the tenderloin in four pieces, crossways. Butterfly all pieces by slicing partially into sides, creating flaps. Spread open pork pieces.
2. Place pork in between cling wrap sheets. Use flat side of meat mallet to pound the pork down to 1/4" thickness. Season with kosher salt ground pepper.
3. Whisk eggs, mustard and the garlic powder together in shallow dish. Place the cracker crumbs in separate shallow dish.
4. Heat 1/4" of oil in sauté pan on med-high. Dip the pork pieces in the egg mixture and allow the excess to drip off. Then dredge them in the cracker crumbs and press to make sure they adhere well.
5. Fry the pork pieces in oil and turn once till meat has a golden brown color, two to four minutes on each side. Add the condiments desired to rolls. Serve.

Wild Rice Salad

This is a Minnesota-centric version of a German slaw recipe that was and is served at many carry-in suppers. The nutty flavor comes from wild rice, and it works quite well with the taste of tangy sauerkraut.

Makes 8 Servings

Cooking + Prep Time: 1 hour 5 minutes + chilling and cooling time

Ingredients:

- 2 x 14-oz. cans of rinsed, drained sauerkraut
- 2/3 cup of wild rice, uncooked
- 3/4 cup of celery, chopped
- 1 peeled, chopped apple, medium
- 3/4 cup of carrot, shredded
- 1/2 cup of red onion, chopped finely

For the dressing

- 1/3 cup of vinegar, cider
- 1/2 cup of sugar, granulated
- 3 tbsp. of oil, canola
- 1/4 tsp. of salt, kosher
- 1/4 tsp. of pepper, ground
- 3 tbsp. of fresh parsley, minced
- 1 tsp. of tarragon, dried
- 3/4 cup of toasted walnuts, chopped

Instructions:

1. Cook the wild rice using instructions on package and allow it to completely cool.

2. Combine the sauerkraut, celery, apples, onions, carrots and rice in large sized bowl. In smaller bowl, whisk first five ingredients for dressing till sugar dissolves and then stir in the herbs. Add this to the sauerkraut mixture and combine by tossing.

3. Cover and refrigerate for four hours or more, allowing the flavors to fully blend. Add and stir in the walnuts and serve.

Cincinnati-Style Chili

This isn't like every other chili recipe. It's made with a sweet concoction featuring ground beef, piled on spaghetti. It can include beans if you want them, but it doesn't have to. Of course, it's loaded with lots of cheddar cheese.

Makes 6 Servings

Cooking + Prep Time: 55 minutes

Ingredients:

- 2 tsp. of sugar, granulated
- 2 tbsp. of chili powder, low sodium
- 1 tsp. of garlic powder, reduced sodium
- 1 1/2 tsp. of cinnamon, ground
- 1 tsp. of salt, kosher
- 1 1/2-lb. of beef, ground
- 1 1/2 cup of onions, chopped
- 2 cups of water, filtered
- 15 oz. of tomato sauce, low sodium
- 8 oz. of cooked spaghetti
- Cheddar cheese shreds

Instructions:

1. Make spaghetti using instructions on package.

2. Mix the sugar, chili powder, garlic powder, cinnamon and kosher salt in small sized bowl. Set the bowl aside.

3. Cook the ground beef with 1 cup onions in a large sized sauce pan over med-high till beef shows no pink. Drain the fat off.

4. Add water, spice blend and the tomato sauce and bring mixture to a boil. Lower heat level to low. Leave uncovered and simmer for 1/2 hour, occasionally stirring.

5. Add chili to top of spaghetti. Top as desired with 1/2 cup of onions, kidney beans and cheese and serve.

Ham Cheese Pudgy Pie

These little pies are a hand-sized treat for adults and kids alike. The pepper jack cheese gives them a bit of a spicy taste, and the sandwiches are melty and warm.

Makes 1 Serving

Cooking + Prep Time: 10 minutes

Ingredients:

- 2 slices of bread, sourdough
- 2 tbsp. of cooked ham, diced
- 2 tbsp. of canned mushrooms, sliced
- 3 tbsp. of pepper jack cheese shreds
- 1 tbsp. of salsa, bottled

Instructions:

1. Place a slice of sourdough bread in pre-greased sandwich iron and top with ham, cheese, mushrooms, salsa and second slice of bread. Close the sandwich iron.
2. Cook over campfire at med-high heat till bread is golden brown in color and the cheese has melted, usually three to six minutes. Turn occasionally while grilling. Serve.

Detroit-Style Coney Dogs

These are not your New York City Coney dogs. The recipe was born in Detroit, and Midwesterners eat these dogs up.

Makes 4 Servings

Cooking + Prep Time: 1 hour 40 minutes

Ingredients:

- 1 lb. of beef, ground
- 1 minced garlic clove
- 1/2 cup of onion, chopped, + extra for garnishing
- 2 tsp. of salt, kosher
- 2 tsp. of pepper, ground
- 1/2 cup of tomato sauce, low sodium
- 3/4 cups of cracker meal
- 2 tsp. of pepper, cayenne
- 1 tbsp. of chili powder
- 1 tsp. of onion powder
- 1 tsp. of garlic powder
- 1 1/2 tsp. of oregano, dried
- 1 1/2 tsp. of thyme, dried
- 1 1/2 tsp. of cumin, ground
- 4 cups of water, filtered
- 4 buns, hot dog
- 4 hot dogs, natural casing
- For garnishing: mustard, yellow

Instructions:

1. In large sized pan on med-high, sauté ground beef, garlic and onions till beef has cooked fully through, usually five to 10 minutes or so. Drain off 1/2 fat. Season as desired. Add tomato sauce. Stir well.

2. Mix cracker meal with spices in small sized bowl. Add this to meat. Cook till cracker meal has browned. Then add water. Simmer for an hour or so. You can add more water if the mixture is too thick. Season as desired again.

3. Preheat oven to 350F. Wrap buns in aluminum foil. Place in oven for 8-10 minutes to warm them.

4. Detroit-style Coney dogs are usually grilled. You can boil or steam them if you prefer. Place cooked hot dog in bun. Top with the chili mixture, onions and mustard. Serve.

Cheesy Potatoes

Your family will love these wonderful potatoes. They are traditionally served at all kinds of Midwestern get-togethers. Make a large batch and serve the leftovers another day.

Makes 12 Servings

Cooking + Prep Time: 1 hour 20 minutes

Ingredients:

- 3 1/2 lbs. of peeled, cubed potatoes
- 1 x 10 1/2-oz. can of undiluted cream of potato soup, condensed
- 1 cup of dip, French onion
- 3/4 cup of milk, 2%
- 2/3 cup of sour cream
- 1 tsp. of minced parsley, fresh + extra as desired
- 1/4 tsp. of salt, kosher
- 1/4 tsp. of pepper, ground
- 1 x 16-oz. pkg. of cubed Velveeta® processed cheese

Instructions:

1. Preheat the oven to 350F. Place the potatoes in Dutch oven and cover with water. Bring to boil. Reduce the heat and leave uncovered. Cook till tender, eight to 12 minutes or so. Drain the potatoes and allow them to cool a bit.

2. Mix the milk, soup, dip, sour cream, kosher salt, ground pepper and parsley in large sized bowl. Fold in cheese and potatoes gently. Transfer to pre-greased 13" x 9" baking dish.

3. Cover dish and bake for 1/2 hour. Uncover and bake till all is heated through and the cheese has melted, usually 15 to 20 minutes or so. Stir and combine well and sprinkle with extra parsley, as desired. Serve.

Tuna Noodle Casserole

This is a dish that parents in the Midwest regularly make for their families. The tuna, noodles, peas and mushrooms make for a filling and tasty weeknight dinner.

Makes 4 Servings

Cooking + Prep Time: 50 minutes

Ingredients:

- 1 tbsp. of oil, olive
- 1 cup of mushrooms, chopped
- 1 tsp. of garlic, crushed
- 2 tbsp. of flour, whole-wheat, + extra if needed
- 1 cup of broth, mushroom
- 3/4 cup of milk, lactose-free + extra if needed
- Kosher salt ground pepper, as desired
- 6 to 8 oz. of cooked egg noodles
- 1 x 5-oz. can of water-packed tuna
- 1/2 cup of peas, organic if available
- 1/2 cup of extra sharp cheddar cheese shreds
- 1 tsp. of Worcestershire sauce, low sodium
- 1 tbsp. of breadcrumbs

Instructions:

1. Preheat oven to 350F.

2. Heat oil in large fry pan on med-low. Add mushrooms and garlic and sauté for five to six minutes. Add flour. Stir till mixed well. Add 1/2 cup milk and broth. Continuously whisk till smooth. Season as desired.

3. Put tuna, cooked noodles, cheese, peas, remaining milk, mushroom sauce and Worcestershire sauce in baking dish. Combine thoroughly. Sprinkle breadcrumbs over the top. Leave uncovered and bake in 350F oven for 20 to 30 minutes. Season as desired. Serve.

Midwest Veggie Pizza

This recipe is a wonderful way to use up any leftover vegetables from the fridge. It's easy to prepare and you can make all kinds of substitutions to tailor it to your family's tastes.

Makes 15 Servings

Cooking + Prep Time: 35 minutes + cooling time

Ingredients:

- 1 x 8-oz. tube of crescent rolls, refrigerated
- 1 1/2 cups of dip, veggie-dill
- 2 chopped carrots, medium
- 1 cup of chopped broccoli, fresh
- 1 cup of chopped tomatoes, seeded
- 4 sliced green onions
- 1 x 2 1/4-oz. can of drained ripe olives, sliced

Instructions:

1. Unroll the dough for the crescent roll into one rectangle. Press on bottom of lightly greased 13" x 9" baking dish. Seal the seams. Bake in 375F oven till golden brown in color, about 10-12 minutes. Then allow to completely cool on wire rack.
2. Spread the dip over crust and sprinkle with broccoli, carrots, onions, tomatoes olives. Slice in squares and serve.

Toasted Cheese Ravioli

This recipe shows the way St. Louis cooks make the dish and it is delicious and unique. It is breaded, then fried, then sprinkled with Parmesan cheese and served with a marinara sauce.

Makes 6 Servings

Cooking + Prep Time: 35 minutes

Ingredients:

- 2 tbsp. of milk, whole
- 1 egg, large
- 3/4 cup of breadcrumbs, Italian seasoned

Optional:

- 1/2 tsp. of salt, kosher
- 1/2 of 25-oz. pkg. of frozen, thawed ravioli, cheese
- To fry: 3 cups of oil, vegetable
- 1 tbsp. of Parmesan cheese, grated
- 1 x 16-oz. jar of spaghetti sauce, low sodium

Instructions:

1. Combine the milk and large egg in small sized bowl. Pour breadcrumbs in shallow bowl. Dip the ravioli in the milk mixture, then coat them with the breadcrumbs.
2. Heat sauce on med. heat in pan till it bubbles. Lower heat level and simmer.
3. Add 2" of oil to large pan. Heat on med. till small breading amount will sizzle and turn brown. Fry the ravioli, several at a time, for one minute per side, till golden in color. Drain them on a plate lined with paper towels. Sprinkle using the Parmesan cheese. Serve promptly with sauce.

Midwestern-Style Chicken Noodle Soup

This is a unique style of chicken noodle soup. It's filled with chicken, veggies and noodles and just a bit of cayenne. Midwest winters can be cold, and this dish will warm you up.

Makes 12 Servings

Cooking + Prep Time: 50 minutes + 5-6 hours slow cooker time

Ingredients:

- 4 ribs of celery, sliced in 1/2" pieces
- 12 baby carrots, fresh, sliced in 1/2" pieces
- 1 tbsp. of minced parsley, fresh
- 3/4 cup of onion, chopped finely
- 1/4 tsp. of pepper, cayenne
- 1/2 tsp. of pepper, ground
- 2 peeled, halved cloves of garlic
- 1 1/2 tsp. of mustard seed
- 1 1/4 lbs. of halved chicken breast, skinless, boneless
- 1 1/4 lbs. of chicken thighs, skinless, boneless
- 4 x 14 1/2-oz. cans of broth, chicken, low sodium
- 1 x 9-oz. pkg. of linguine, refrigerated
- **Optional:** extra parsley and ground pepper, as desired

Instructions:

1. Combine first six ingredients in large slow cooker. Place the garlic and mustard seed on two layers of cheesecloth. Then bring up the corners. Tie with string, forming a bag and place the bag in your slow cooker. Add the broth and chicken. Cover. Cook on the low setting till meat becomes tender, five to six hours or so.

2. Discard the spice bag and remove the chicken. Allow it to cool a bit. Stir the linguine into the soup. Cover slow cooker. Cook on the high setting till tender, 1/2 hour or so. Cut the chicken in pieces. Return it to the soup. Heat it through. Sprinkle using additional parsley and pepper, as desired, and serve.

Midwestern-Style Swedish Meatballs

Midwesterners got Swedish meatballs straight from the source, from immigrants from Scandinavian countries. These are a bit tangy and creamy and you'll want more!

Makes 4 Servings

Cooking + Prep Time: 45 minutes

Ingredients:

- 4 tbsp. of breadcrumbs, white, fresh
- 4 tbsp. of water or milk
- 8 oz. of beef or veal mince
- 8 oz. of pork mince
- 2 tbsp. of onion, grated
- 1 lightly beaten egg, large
- 3-4 crushed allspice
- As desired: kosher salt ground pepper, WHITE
- To fry: 2 tbsp. of butter, unsalted
- 2 cups of stock, beef
- 2 tbsp. of corn starch, mixed with a bit of filtered water
- 1/2 tsp. of soy sauce, low sodium
- Black pepper, ground, as desired
- 2 tbsp. of cream, heavy

Instructions:

1. Pour breadcrumbs in large sized bowl. Add water or milk and allow the crumbs to sit and absorb liquid for five minutes or so.

2. Add both types of mince, along with egg, onions, allspice seasoning. Use your hands to mix evenly. Do not over-mix it.

3. Roll mixture into balls of 1 tbsp. each. Repeat till all mixture is used up. You should have 25-30 meatballs or so.

4. Heat 1 tbsp. butter in fry pan on med-high till butter has stopped sizzling. Fry 1/2 of meatballs and shake pan frequently when they are first added. When browned nicely, turn heat down. Cook for 10 more minutes. Remove meatballs and keep them warm.

5. Add 1 more tbsp. butter. Fry remainder of meatballs as you did the first batch in step 4.

6. When all meatballs have been cooked, remove pan from heat. Add stock and corn starch mixture. Stir well and reheat. Simmer for about five minutes. Add soy sauce, cream and seasoning. Heat for a couple more minutes while continuously stirring. Serve.

Wisconsin Burgers

Wisconsin residents love dairy products, and many are made locally. These burgers are topped with a pat of butter. Restaurants in the Midwest and other areas have picked up on "Butter Burgers", and they are very popular.

Makes 4 Servings

Cooking + Prep Time: 35 minutes

Ingredients:

- 1 lb. of ground beef, lean
- 1/2 tsp. of salt, seasoned
- 1/2 tsp. of pepper, ground
- 1/2 lb. of mushrooms, fresh
- 2 tbsp. + 4 tsp. of butter, unsalted
- 4 split buns, hamburger

Toppings, Optional: lettuce leaves, sliced tomatoes, sliced dill pickles, mustard and ketchup

Instructions:

1. Sprinkle the beef with the seasoned salt ground pepper. Pulse the mushrooms in food processor till chopped finely. Add them to beef and mix lightly. Shape into four patties, about 1/2-inch thick.

2. Heat 2 tbsp. of butter on med. heat in large sized skillet. Add the burgers. Cook for six to eight minutes per side and baste with butter, till internal thermometer reads 160F. Remove them from heat and keep them warm. Add the tops of buns to the skillet and toast them till golden brown in color.

3. Transfer the burgers to bottom buns. Top them with 1 tsp. of butter each. Add desired toppings. Replace the tops of buns and serve.

Potato Cheese Pierogi

Many Polish immigrants settled in the Midwest, mostly in states including Minnesota, Ohio and Illinois. So, these pierogis are original to the Polish but are now Midwestern US favorites, too.

Makes 4 Servings

Cooking + Prep Time: 1 hour 40 minutes + 1/2 hour resting time

Ingredients:

For pierogi

- 2 eggs, large
- 4 cups of baking mix (like Bisquick®)
- 2/3 cup of water, warm
- 1/2 cup of sour cream, reduced fat
- 1 tsp. of salt, kosher

For filling

- 2 lbs. peeled, cubed potatoes
- 1 cup of cheddar cheese, sharp, grated
- 1 chopped onion, large
- 4 tbsp. of butter, unsalted
- 1 chopped onion, large
- To garnish: sour cream

Instructions:

1. To prepare pierogi, combine all the ingredients. Knead till blended well.

2. Let the dough rest, covered, for 1/2 hour, covered with damp towel.

3. Divide the dough into eight pieces. Work on one piece of dough at a time. Leave remainder of dough covered. Roll each piece to 1/8" thickness. Cut them into three-inch rounds.

4. To prepare filling, peel cube the potatoes. Cook them in salted, boiling water till tender.

5. Melt butter in a skillet. Fry the onions till they are caramelized.

6. Drain the potatoes. Add 1/2 onions plus cheddar cheese. Combine well. Season as desired and allow mixture to cool.

7. Place 1 heaping tsp. filling onto rounds. Moisten edges with filtered water. Fold them over. Seal by pressing together. Bring large pot of salted water to boil.

8. Add the pierogi. Be sure not to crowd them. Cook till they float to top. Then let them cook for three or four more minutes. Drizzle with butter. Serve.

Grilled Sweet Corn

The heartland of America has lots of sweet corn freshly picked and available in season. That's why the recipe is cooked so often during the summer months. The cumin, parsley and chili powder bring out the just-picked flavor of the corn.

Makes 8 Servings

Cooking + Prep Time: 40 minutes

Ingredients:

- 8 husk-on sweet corn ears, large
- 6 tbsp. of softened butter, unsalted
- 1 tbsp. of minced parsley, fresh
- 1 tsp. of salt, garlic
- 1-2 tsp. of chili powder
- 1/1 tsp. of cumin, ground

Instructions:

1. Place the corn in a large stock pot covered with cold water and soak for 20-25 minutes.
2. Mix the remainder of ingredients. Drain the corn. Peel husks back carefully to within an inch of the bottom. Remove silk.
3. Spread the corn with your butter mixture. Rewrap in the husks. Tie using kitchen string.
4. Grill the corn on covered grill on med. heat till tender, about 25 to 30 minutes. Be sure to turn it often so it grills evenly.
5. Remove corn from grill. Cut the string. Peel husks back and serve.

Beef Cheese Goulash

This simple recipe will create a dinner that pleases everyone in the house, family and guests alike. Everyone seems to love the mixture of ground beef, noodles, cheese, tomatoes and tasty seasonings.

Makes 8 Servings

Cooking + Prep Time: 1 hour 10 minutes

Ingredients:

- 2 pounds of beef, ground
- 3 tsp. of garlic, minced
- 3 cups of water, filtered
- 2 x 15-ounce cans of tomato sauce, low sodium
- 2 x 15-ounce cans of tomatoes, diced
- 3 bay leaves, medium
- 3 tbsp. of soy sauce, reduced sodium
- 1 tbsp. of salt, seasoned
- 2 tbsp. of seasoning, Italian
- 2 cups of uncooked macaroni, elbow
- 1 cup of cheddar cheese shreds

Instructions:

1. Sauté the ground beef in a skillet on med-high till cooked fully. Drain well. Add the garlic. Sauté for five minutes more. Add the water, diced tomatoes, tomato sauce, bay leaves, Italian seasoning, soy sauce seasoned salt and stir well. Then cover and cook for 18-20 minutes.

2. Add uncooked macaroni to the skillet. Stir thoroughly. Cover. Simmer for 1/2 hour. Turn heat off. Remove bay leaves. Add cheddar cheese, stir and serve.

Midwest-Style Pot Pie

The pot pies you see in the frozen food section of the grocery are nothing like these wonderful, homemade pot pies. These are like crust-enveloped comfort food for adults and kids alike.

Makes 6 Servings

Cooking + Prep Time: 35 minutes

- 2 tbsp. of oil, canola
- 1 chopped onion, medium
- 1/2 cup of flour, all-purpose
- 1 tsp. of seasoning, poultry
- 1 x 14 1/2-oz. can of broth, chicken
- 3/4 cup of milk, 2%
- 3 cups of cubed chicken, cooked
- 2 cups of frozen, thawed mixed vegetables
- 1 sheet of pie crust, refrigerated

Instructions:

1. Preheat the oven to 450F.

2. Heat the oil on med-high in large sized pan. Add the onion. Stir while cooking till it is tender. Add and stir in the poultry seasoning and flour till blended well. Whisk in milk and broth gradually.

3. Bring mixture to boil and stir constantly. Stir for two or three more minutes, till it thickens. Add and stir in vegetables and chicken.

4. Transfer mixture to lightly-greased 9-inch pie plate (deep dish) and place the crust over the filling. Trim and seal, then flute the edges. Cut small slits in the crust.

5. Bake pot pie for 18-20 minutes, till filling is bubbling and crust is a golden brown color. Serve.

Midwesterners love a good dessert, too! Here are some of their finest offerings...

Midwest Cherry Pie

This pie uses tart cherries for a unique taste. This recipe includes a crust made from scratch with real cream cheese. It's SO delicious!

Makes 10 Servings

Cooking + Prep Time: 1 hour 45 minutes

Ingredients:

- 2 x 14 1/2-ounce cans of undrained cherries, tart, pitted
- 1 cup + 1 tsp. of sugar, granulated
- 1/4 tsp. of almond extract, pure
- 1/4 cup of corn starch
- 6 ounces of softened cream cheese
- 3/4 cup of softened butter, unsalted
- 2 1/4 cups of flour, all-purpose

Instructions:

1. Drain the cherries and reserve one cup of their liquid. Mix a cup of sugar and the corn starch in sauce pan. Add the cherries and their reserved liquid and stir.

2. Cook over med-high for 10-12 minutes, till boiling. Cook till mixture thickens, while constantly stirring. Stir while cooking for one minute and allow to completely cool. Add and stir in the extract.

3. Heat the oven to 375F. Beat the butter and cream cheese in large sized bowl using mixer till blended well.

4. Add flour gradually to cream cheese mixture and mix thoroughly after each amount added. The dough should be crumbly in texture. Shape into two balls and flatten them a bit. Roll out 1/2 dough on a floured work surface to an 11" circle. Place this in a nine-inch pie plate and fill it with the cherry mixture.

5. Roll out the remainder of dough to another 11" circle. Cut it into 10 strips of 1/2" width. Next, weave the dough strips over the filling, creating a lattice design. Fold the edge of the bottom crust over strip ends. Sprinkle the top with the remainder of the sugar.

6. Bake for 35 - 40 minutes, till filling is bubbly and hot and crust has turned golden brown in color. Serve.

Rainbow Gelatin

Rainbow gelatin is a signature dessert for many of the older generation in the Midwest and many younger parents, as well. It's often served and loved for spring and summer cookouts and parties.

Makes 12-16 Servings

Cooking + Prep Time: 25 minutes + 9 hours chilling time

Ingredients:

- 6 x 3-oz. boxes of gelatin: one box each of yellow, orange, red, blue, green and purple
- 6 cups of water, boiling
- 3 cups of water, cold

For white layers

- 4 cups of milk, 2%
- 1 cup of water, boiling
- 4 envelopes of gelatin, Knox®
- 24 oz. of yogurt, vanilla
- 1 cup of sugar, granulated
- 4 tsp. of vanilla extract, pure

Instructions:

1. Set out six small-sized bowls. Mix a box of gelatin with a cup of boiling water 1/2 cup cold water in each bowl. Do all colors at same time.

2. Heat milk in pan on low heat till lukewarm. In large sized bowl, mix 1 cup of boiling water with Knox® gelatin. Whisk well till gelatin dissolves completely. Add yogurt, warm milk, vanilla extract and sugar. Whisk till combined well and fully smooth with zero lumps.

3. Pour first color of gelatin into 13" x 9" pan. Refrigerate till it sets. Once it sets, gently pour 1 1/2 cups of yogurt mixture on the top of the first color. Return to fridge for 45 more minutes, till set fully.

4. Repeat this step with remaining gelatin colors and the yogurt mixture till you have used the last color. You'll probably have yogurt mixture left over. When fully finished with colors, refrigerate for an hour or more. Store in fridge till serving.

Amish Cookies

There are many Amish groups living in the Midwest. This is one of their favorite recipes, and a favorite among other Midwesterners, as well.

Makes 60 Cookies

Cooking + Prep Time: 1 hour 5 minutes

Ingredients:

- 1 cup of oil, vegetable
- 1 cup of softened butter, unsalted
- 1 cup of sugar, granulated
- 1 cup of sugar, confectioner's
- 2 eggs, large
- 1/2 tsp. of vanilla extract, pure
- 4 1/2 cups of flour, all-purpose
- 3/4 tsp. of cream of tartar
- 1 tsp. of baking soda

Instructions:

1. Preheat oven to 375F. Grease the baking sheets.
2. Mix oil, butter and both sugars in large sized bowl till you have a smooth consistency. Beat eggs in one after another. Add and stir in vanilla.
3. Combine baking soda, flour and the cream of tartar. Stir it into sugar mixture till barely combined. Don't overmix. Drop the dough in teaspoonfuls on greased baking sheets.
4. Bake cookies for eight to 10 minutes at 375F till bottoms brown lightly. Remove from cookie sheets and cool them on wire racks. Serve.

Apple Crisp

This is a favorite dessert recipe in the US Midwest. The apples are combined with brown sugar, spices and lemon, and topped with a crumbly, wonderful crisp.

Makes 8-10 Servings

Cooking + Prep Time: 50 minutes

Ingredients:

For apple filling

- 6 cored, sliced large apples, honey crisp
- 1 1/2 lemon, juice only
- 3/4 cup of sugar, granulated
- 3/4 cup of sugar, brown
- 6 tbsp. of flour, all-purpose
- 1 1/2 tsp. of cinnamon, ground
- 1/4 tsp. of allspice
- 1/4 tsp. of nutmeg, ground
- 3 tsp. of vanilla extract, pure
- Several pinches of salt, kosher

For topping

- 1 cup of flour, all-purpose
- 1 cup of rolled oats, old-fashioned
- 3/4 cup of sugar, brown
- 1 tsp. of cinnamon, ground
- 1 large pinch salt, kosher
- 1/2 cup of cold, cubed butter, unsalted

Instructions:

1. Heat the oven to 375F. Grease 13" x 9" baking dish lightly.
2. Add the sliced apples to large bowl. Squeeze the lemon juice over the top. Add remainder of filling ingredients to bowl. Using your hands, toss apples and coat them evenly in mixture.
3. Dump the apples in pre-greased baking dish.
4. Pour the topping ingredients in medium sized bowl. Combine the ingredients. Break butter gently into pieces about the size of peas.
5. Spread the topping in one even layer over apples.
6. Bake for 1/2 hour, till apples are tender when pierced with a fork, and crisp topping is deep golden brown in color. Serve.

Midwest's Finest Chocolate Cake

This cake has been called the richest, moistest, most chocolaty cake in the Midwest. Use prepared frosting or your own recipe for this classic cake.

Makes 12-16 Servings

Cooking + Prep Time: 55 minutes + 1/2 hour standing time

Ingredients:

- 3 eggs, large
- 3/4 cup of butter, softened
- 2 cups of flour, all-purpose
- 3/4 cup of cocoa powder, unsweetened
- 3/4 tsp. of baking powder
- 1 tsp. of baking soda
- 1/2 tsp. of salt, kosher
- 2 cups of sugar, granulated
- 1 tsp. of vanilla, pure
- 1 1/2 cups of milk, whole
- Chocolate Sour Cream Frosting, prepared

Instructions:

1. Allow the eggs and butter to sit at room temperature for 1/2 hour. Grease bottoms of 2 x 8" square cake pans lightly. Line pans with wax or parchment paper. Grease, then flour sides of pans and paper lightly. Set the pans aside.

2. Stir cocoa powder, flour, baking powder, baking soda and kosher salt together in medium sized bowl. Set it aside.

3. Beat the butter on med-high with electric mixer for 25-30 seconds in large sized bowl. Add the sugar gradually, roughly 1/4 cup after another and beat on med. speed till combined well. Scrape bowl sides and beat on med. for two minutes more. Add the eggs, one after another and beat after each one is added. Beat in the vanilla.

4. Add milk and flour mixture alternately to the beaten mixture. Beat using low speed until barely combined after each milk/flour mixture addition. Then beat on med or high speed for 20 more seconds. Evenly spread the batter into your prepared pans.

5. Bake at 350F for 35-40 minutes. Cool layers in their pans for about 10 minutes and then remove them. Peel paper off. Thoroughly cool on wire cooling racks. Frost, slice and serve.

Conclusion

This Midwest U. S. cookbook has shown you…

How to use different ingredients to affect unique Midwest American tastes in dishes both well-known and rare.

How can you include Midwestern cuisine in your home recipes?

You can…

- Make tasty quiche or delicious blueberry pancakes, which I imagine everyone knows about. They are just as tasty as you have heard, for breakfast.

- Learn to cook with fresh vegetables, like peas, corn, beans and more, which are widely used in the Midwest US. Find them in local food markets.

- Enjoy making the delectable freshwater fish dishes of the Midwest, including trout and carp. Fish is readily available in the region, and there are SO many ways to make it great.

- Make dishes using cherries and apples, which are often used in Midwest cooking.

- Make various types of desserts like cherry pie and decadent chocolate cake that will tempt your family's sweet tooth.

Have fun experimenting! Enjoy the results!

Author's Afterthoughts

Thanks ever so much to each of my cherished readers for investing the time to read this book!

I know you could have picked from many other books, but you chose this one. So, a big thanks for reading all the way to the end. If you enjoyed this book or received value from it, I'd like to ask you for a favor. Please take a few minutes to **post an honest and heartfelt review on** *Amazon.com.* Your support does make a difference and helps to benefit other people.

Thanks!

Julia Chiles

About the Author

Julia Chiles

(1951-present)

Julia received her culinary degree from Le Counte' School of Culinary Delights in Paris, France. She enjoyed cooking more than any of her former positions. She lived in Montgomery, Alabama most of her life. She married Roger

Chiles and moved with him to Paris as he pursued his career in journalism. During the time she was there, she joined several cooking groups to learn the French cuisine, which inspired her to attend school and become a great chef.

Julia has achieved many awards in the field of food preparation. She has taught at several different culinary schools. She is in high demand on the talk show circulation, sharing her knowledge and recipes. Julia's favorite pastime is learning new ways to cook old dishes.

Julia is now writing cookbooks to add to her long list of achievements. The present one consists of favorite recipes as well as a few culinary delights from other cultures. She expands everyone's expectations on how to achieve wonderful dishes and not spend a lot of money. Julia firmly believes a wonderful dish can be prepare out of common household staples.

If anyone is interested in collecting Julia's cookbooks, check out your local bookstores and online. They are a big seller whatever venue you choose to purchase from.

www.ingramcontent.com/pod-product-compliance
Lightning Source LLC
Chambersburg PA
CBHW020118180726
47992CB00019B/1017